Travels Across America

The Southeast

Elspeth Leacock

PICTURE CREDITS
Cover Baron Wolman/Stone; page 1, 11, 19, 29 (second from top)
Medford Taylor/National Geographic Society, Image Collection (NGSIC);
page 2-3, 21 (top), 28 (bottom) Melissa Farlow/NGSIC; page 4-5 Phyllis
Picardi/Stock Boston; page 5 (inset), 9 (inset), 24 Peter Cade/Stone;
page 6-7 Marc Muench/Stone; page 7 (top), 13 (top), 21 (bottom), 30
(third from top) Richard T. Nowitz/ NGSIC; page 7 (bottom) David R.
Fraizer/Photolibrary/Folio, Inc; page 8 Dashun Guo/NGSIC; page 8
(inset), 10, 28 (third from top) Chris Johns/NGSIC; page 9 Thad
Samuels Abell II/NGSIC; page 10 (inset) Jeff Greenberg/Rainbow; page
11 (inset) Otis Imboden Jr. Inc/NGSIC; page 12-13 Eric Tucker/Stone;
page 13 (bottom) Tessa Codrington/Stone; page 15 Bob S.
Sacha/NGSIC; page 16, 29 (third from top) William Albert Allard/NGSIC;
page 17 James P. Blair/NGSIC; page 18, 22 (inset), 23 (bottom), 26, 29
(top) Raymond K. Gehman/NGSIC; page 20-21 Dick S.
Durrance/NGSIC; page 22 Ensign Cameras/NGSIC; page 23 (top) Annie
Griffiths Belt/NGSIC; page 25 (top) Joel Sartore/ NGSIC; page 25
(inset), 27 (top) Bettmann/CORBIS; page 27 (bottom) Daniel R.
Westergren/NGSIC; page 28 (top) Jeff Greenberg/ Folio, Inc.; page 28,
30 (second from top) Randy Olson/NGSIC; page 29 (bottom) Everett C.
Johnson/Folio, Inc; page 30 (top) Randy Wells/Stone; page 30 (bottom)
Rich LaSalle/Stone; back cover (top to bottom) Cosmo Condina/Stone;
Art Wolfe/Stone; Eric Meola/Image Bank; Joel Sartore/NGSIC, Terry
Donnelly/Stone

Produced through the worldwide resources of the National Geographic
Society, John M. Fahey, Jr., President and Chief Executive Officer;
Gilbert M. Grosvenor, Chairman of the Board; Nina D. Hoffman,
Executive Vice President and President, Books and School Publishing.

Cover: Fort Lauderdale, Florida
Title page: Cape Hatteras, North Carolina
Contents page: Okefenokee National Wildlife Refuge, Georgia

PREPARED BY NATIONAL GEOGRAPHIC SCHOOL PUBLISHING
Ericka Markman, Vice President; Steve Mico, Editorial Director;
Marianne Hiland, Editorial Manager; Anita Schwartz, Project Editor;
Tara Peterson, Editorial Assistant; Jim Hiscott, Design Manager; Linda
McKnight, Art Director; Diana Bourdrez, Photo Research; Sean
Philpotts, Production Coordinator; Matt Wascavage, Manager of
Publishing Services.

MANUFACTURING AND QUALITY MANAGEMENT
Christopher A. Liedel, Chief Financial Officer; Phillip L. Schlosser,
Director; Clifton M. Brown III, Manager.

PROGRAM DEVELOPMENT
Gare Thompson Associates, Inc.

BOOK DESIGN
Herman Adler Design

Published by the National Geographic Society
Washington, D.C. 20036-4688

Product No. 4J41230

ISBN-13: 978-0-7922-8699-8

Printed in Canada

11 10 09 08 07 06
10 9 8 7 6 5 4 3

Table of Contents

Hello!

or Hi y'all, as some say here in the Southeast. My name is Kendra. I will be your guide as we explore the Southeast region. We will visit the states of Kentucky, West Virginia, Virginia, Tennessee, North Carolina, South Carolina, Georgia, Alabama, Mississippi, Louisiana, Arkansas, and Florida.

We'll be doing a lot of traveling. But don't worry. On this tour you can stop anytime just by shutting the book. You can eat a snack or take a walk. When you are ready to continue our adventure, I'll be right here.

First, we'll look at the land of the Southeast. I'll show you all my favorite places. Then we'll see what kind of jobs people have in this region. Finally, we'll meet some of the people of the Southeast. They'll show us how they live and some of the things they like to do for fun. I hope y'all enjoy the trip. Let's go!

Smoky Mountains

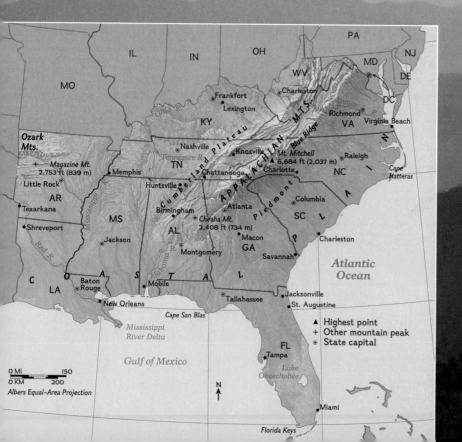

IL
IN
OH
PA
MO
WV
MD
NJ
Charleston
DC
DE

Frankfort
Lexington

Richmond
VA
Virginia Beach

KY

Ozark
Mts.

Nashville
Knoxville
Mt. Mitchell
6,684 ft (2,037 m)
Raleigh

+ Magazine Mt.
2,753 ft (839 m)
Memphis
TN
Chattanooga
Charlotte
NC
Cape
Hatteras

Little Rock

Huntsville

AR

Texarkana
Atlanta
Columbia

Shreveport
MS
Birmingham
+ Cheaha Mt.
2,408 ft (734 m)
SC

Jackson
AL
Macon
Charleston

Montgomery
GA
Savannah
Atlantic
Ocean

C
A
Baton
Rouge
Mobile

LA
New Orleans
Tallahassee
Jacksonville
St. Augustine

Cape San Blas

Mississippi
River Delta
▲ Highest point
+ Other mountain peak
◉ State capital

FL

Gulf of Mexico
Tampa
Lake
Okeechobee

0 MI   150
0 KM   200
N
↑

Albers Equal-Area Projection

Miami

Florida Keys

Chapter 1

The Land

The Most

The Southeast has more warm **wetlands** than any other region. Its long shoreline gives us beautiful sandy beaches to enjoy.

The Oldest

The Appalachian Mountains are the oldest mountains in the United States. They were formed over 250 million years ago. That was before the age of the dinosaurs!

The Highest and the Lowest

- The highest mountain in the region is Mt. Mitchell in North Carolina. It is part of the Appalachian Mountains.

- Florida is the flattest, lowest state. Millions of years ago the land now known as Florida was sea bottom.

Miami Beach, Florida

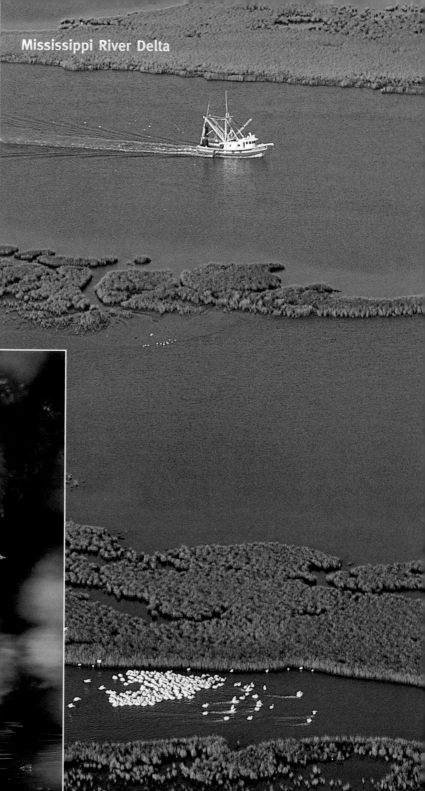

Mississippi River Delta

IN THE OLD DAYS

Naming the Mississippi
When European explorers reached the Mississippi River, they asked the Ojibwa people living there what the river was called. "Mici zibi" they answered, which means "great river."

Egret in the Everglades

8

The Mighty Mississippi River

We're going to begin our trip at the **mouth** of the Mississippi River. Here, the fresh water of the river mixes with the salty water of the Gulf of Mexico.

Have you ever looked at a river's mouth before? You won't see any big teeth. But in this river's mouth you will see lots of mud—about 13,000 square miles of it. And it was all brought here by the river. About 400 million tons of mud are carried here every year from farmlands 2,000 miles away. That's how this watery **landform** called the Mississippi Delta gets its rich, dark soil.

Water in this **delta** region does not always drain away. As a result, wetlands, called **marshes**, stretch out in every direction! Here you see only a few trees. They grow only where the ground is higher, but don't try to sit in their shade. You'll sink up to your waist in mud. Alligators just love these marshes. So do all the wading birds. With their long legs and long necks, they are able to wade in the water and find shrimp, crawfish, and other sorts of fish to eat. Under water, this quiet place is teeming with life.

The Appalachian Mountains

There are many other landforms to see, so let's move on to the Cumberland Plateau. A **plateau** is an area of flat land that is higher than the land around it. But not much is left of the flat top here. It has been **eroded**, or worn away, leaving deep valleys and steep hills.

Up ahead are the Appalachian Mountains. These mountains are not very tall, only 2,000 to 6,000 feet high. That is because the Appalachians are very old and have worn away. When they were young, the Appalachians were towering snowcapped mountains. That was over 250 million years ago!

Kendra's Picks

A Long, Long Trail

Would you like to hike from Georgia all the way north to Maine? You can by following the Appalachian Trail all along the Appalachian Mountains. Well, actually you don't have to hike the whole way. You can hike just as far as you like and enjoy the beautiful mountain views.

Everglades

Kendra's Picks

Okefenokee Swamp

The Okefenokee Swamp in Georgia is a wild place to visit. I saw the eyes and nose of an alligator floating above the water. The tip of its nose was about nine inches from its eyes. The ranger told me that means the alligator was about nine feet long! Thousands of alligators float around this swamp. Do you know what else floats here? Whole islands covered with trees, bushes, and vines drift from one spot to another. It's easy to get lost in the Okefenokee.

Rolling Hills and Flat Plains

On the eastern side of the Appalachian Mountains is the Piedmont region. *Piedmont* is a French word that means "foothills." And that is just what the Piedmont is, gently rolling hills at the foot of the mountains.

As we travel east, the land gets flat. We're now on the **coastal plain.** If you look at the map on page 6, you'll see that this landform stretches from Virginia to Florida along the Atlantic and the Gulf coasts to Louisiana.

In some areas, these plains are so flat that water hardly moves at all. So here you'll find more wetlands. If you're beginning to think that the Southeast has lots of water and wetlands, you are right! Have you ever heard of the Great Dismal Swamp? Well, it's right here in Virginia and North Carolina. You saw marshes at the Mississippi Delta, but a **swamp** is a different kind of wetland.

A marsh is grassy with just a few trees. It is a bright and sunny place. A swamp is filled with trees and hanging vines. It's a dark and mysterious place. In the dim light under the trees and the tangle of vines, raccoons, bobcats, and even bears live. What a great setting for a scary movie!

Assateague Island ponies

Islands

The Southeast has hundreds of islands, too. My favorite is Assateague Island off the Atlantic coast.

Assateague Island is a sand dune, a long thin hill of sand. It is called a **barrier island** because it acts like a barrier, or wall, protecting the mainland from rough ocean waves. The island is famous for its wild ponies. Ponies have lived here for hundreds of years, wild and free.

Further south in the tropical waters off Florida, you will find a special kind of island called a **key**. Keys are made from **coral**, limestone skeletons formed by tiny sea animals. Sometimes masses of coral get so big that they rise above the water, forming coral islands.

As you can see, the Southeast is made up of different land areas. Now that we've toured the wetlands, plains, and hills of the region, it's time to travel its highways and waterways.

Let's see how the people living here use the land and the many resources in the region to make a living. Let's find out why the Southeast is one of the fastest growing regions in the country.

Kendra's Picks

An Underwater Park

To see why the Florida Keys are special, go to John Pennekamp Coral Reef State Park. It's the nation's first underwater park. You can ride in a glass-bottomed boat to see a living coral reef. More than 500 different kinds of tropical fish live there.

Chapter 2

The Economy

The First

The first tabasco sauce was created in Louisiana. It is made from little red hot peppers that just love the hot and humid climate.

The Only

Crater of Diamonds State Park in Murfreesboro, Arkansas, is the only diamond field in the world where you can prospect for and keep any diamonds you find.

The Most

- Whatever you are wearing could be from North Carolina. Mills there produce more cloth than any other state.

- Florida produces about seven out of every ten oranges in the United States and eight of every ten grapefruits.

A Two-Lane Water Highway

Barges and small boats have their own highway, protected from the big waves out in the Gulf. It is a two-lane water highway called the Gulf Intracoastal Waterway. It stretches from Florida all the way to Texas. Petroleum and petroleum products are carried along this highway.

Container Ships and Oil Rigs

We will begin our tour of the **economy** of the Southeast along its waterways. Remember, the economy is the way a region uses its natural resources, goods, and services.

Out here in the Gulf of Mexico, the world's largest **gulf**, everything seems big. A gulf is a large area of sea that is partly surrounded by land. Look at the size of the ships here. These are container ships. They carry huge metal containers stacked like blocks. Inside those containers is everything you can imagine, from bananas to batteries.

In the Gulf, you'll also see giant drilling rigs. Do you know what they are doing? They are drilling for oil deep below the ocean bottom. Oil is an important resource in the Southeast.

While we are here in the Gulf, let's stop off at one of the world's busiest ports, New Orleans.

Port of Trade

Do you know why there are so many ships here? New Orleans is located along the Mississippi River about 100 miles from where the river flows into the Gulf of Mexico. Trace the Mississippi River on a U.S. map. You'll see that the river and rivers that flow into it—its **tributaries**—reach every region of the country.

Here's a barge full of wheat from Ohio. It was towed down the Ohio River to Mississippi to New Orleans. Now the wheat will be loaded onto a freighter bound for Europe or Africa. Wheat and other foods from the Midwest are important crops that we **export** to other countries. See that freighter from Brazil? It brought in a full load of coffee beans. The beans are being unloaded. Then they'll be taken away to be roasted the way people here like them. The beans have been **imported**, or brought into the United States from another country.

More than 6,000 boats pass through the port of New Orleans every year. About 94,000 people work loading and unloading all of that **cargo**. Let's follow some of this cargo and head out onto the highway to see more of the Southeast's economy.

Weirton
Wheeling
Iron and steel
Coal

PA

NJ

IL

IN

OH

MD

DE

WV

Charleston
Chemicals

VA

DC

MO

Louisville
Chemicals
Food
Machinery

Huntington
Coal

Richmond

Paper

Lynchburg

Clothes

Shipbuilding

Electronics

Newport News

Norfolk

Coal

Coal

Roanoke

Coal

Coal

KY

Greensboro
Winston-
Salem

Burlington

Clothes

Nashville

Food
Autos

Food
Clothes

Zinc
Knoxville

Durham

Electronics

AR

TN

High Point

Textiles

Food
Phosphate

Textiles

Memphis

Chattanooga

Chemicals

Gastonia

Charlotte

NC

Little Rock
Chemicals
Bauxite
Aluminum

Florence

Decatur

Huntsville
Aircraft

Greenville

Spartanburg

SC

Textiles

Birmingham
Iron and
steel

Atlanta
Food
Clothes
Aircraft

North Augusta
Textiles
Chemicals

Oil

MS

AL

GA

LA

Columbus
Food
Textiles

Chemicals

Baton
Rouge

Oil
refining

Mobile

Paper

Paper

Paper

Savannah

Oil
refining

Clothes
Pascagoula

Pensacola

New Orleans
Shipbuilding

Jacksonville

Oil

Paper
Food

Phosphate

FL

Orlando

Atlantic
Ocean

Food

Gulf of
Mexico

St. Petersburg

Tampa
Electronics
Chemicals

N

Electronics

0 MI   150
0 KM   200

Albers Equal-Area Projection

Food
Clothes

Miami

Cotton field in Mississippi

Fields of Many Colors

As we travel the highways, the fields on each side of the highway change colors. They look like a patchwork quilt! There are green fields of rice and tobacco and golden fields of soybeans. There are fields filled with white puffs of cotton and tall fields of corn. The fruit orchards are even taller.

All this talk of food makes me hungry. How about stopping for a snack? I'll start with a bag of peanuts. It's my favorite snack. Peanuts are one of the most important crops grown in this region. To grow, peanuts need months and months of warm days and nights. That is just what they get here, a long growing season. They are grown from Alabama to Virginia. But Georgia is the number one state for growing peanuts.

Do you remember which state is number one for growing oranges? Here's a hint. Oranges grow best where summers are long and winters are cool but rarely freezing. If you said Florida, you're right.

Fields of Coal

Now we're ready to visit the coalfields in Kentucky, West Virginia, and Tennessee. Our first stop is Bullpush Mountain. This was the first mountaintop-removal mine in West Virginia. Now read that again—slower: mountaintop-removal mine! That's why there is only a meadow here now. The mine is gone, but so is the mountain! Now it's a grassy plateau!

Long ago, coal miners used picks and shovels to carve out coal from inside a mountain. But now explosives are used to break up the mountain. Then huge—and I mean HUGE—shovels pick up and carry away the coal. There are still underground mines, too. Let's go see one.

Here in Bald Knob, West Virginia, miners work underground. They use a big machine that can dig 12 tons of coal every minute and load it onto a belt that carries it out of the mine! With machines like that, a whole train of coal cars can be loaded up pretty quickly.

Peanuts— An American Favorite

Americans love peanuts. We eat over one billion pounds of peanut butter every year and another one billion pounds of peanuts as snacks.

IN THE
OLD
DAYS

Made by Hand

In the days before there were any factories, people made a lot of things by hand. You need great skill to sew a fine quilt by hand or carve a beautiful musical instrument from wood. In Appalachia, people became well known for these skills and still are to this day.

Textiles and Tables

A lot of the coal is burned to create electric power. That's where we are headed next, to a power plant. You know what electricity is used for, right? Some is used to power our lights and television sets. But most of it is used to make furniture and cars and baseball caps and a whole lot more. Making something, usually with machines, is called **manufacturing**.

The Southeast is the number one region in manufacturing **textiles**, or cloth. They manufacture things from wood, too, such as tables, chairs, and beds. The Southeast is also number one in manufacturing furniture. Look at the map on page 15. What other things in your home or school may have been manufactured in the Southeast?

It's been a long trip. You're probably ready to slow down for a while. How about going to the beach?

Tourists From Two to Ninety

With all that water and coastland, the Southeast is a region of beautiful beaches. In summer, people enjoy swimming in the waters of the Atlantic Ocean off the coast of Virginia and the Carolinas. In winter, about 40 million tourists flock to the state of Florida alone.

But the Southeast has more than just sunshine and beaches. Did you ever want to be an astronaut? You can train to be one at the U.S. Space and Rocket Center's camp in Huntsville, Alabama. Did you ever wish you had been one of the early American settlers? Then relive American history at Williamsburg's colonial village in Virginia. Ever make a model? At Dollywood in Tennessee you can watch an Appalachian woodworker carve a musical instrument by hand. You can also ride the rides at one of the great theme parks in the region.

Now that we've seen what people in the Southeast do for a living, let's find out more about them. Let's find about their history and **culture**, their way of life.

Colonial Williamsburg

Churchill Downs, home of the Kentucky Derby

The Culture

St. Augustine Fort

The Oldest

- The oldest permanent European settlement is St. Augustine, Florida. The Spanish founded it in 1565.
- The first English **colony** in the Americas was on Roanoke Island in Virginia. It was founded in 1583 by Sir Walter Raleigh. But its settlers disappeared. No one knows what happened to them.

The First

In the 1700s, Charleston, South Carolina, was the wealthiest city in the South. It had the first public library, the first theater, and the first museum in the colonies.

The Most

More Presidents of the United States were born in Virginia than in any other state. The total is eight so far: George Washington, Thomas Jefferson, James Madison, James Monroe, William Henry Harrison, John Tyler, Zachary Taylor, and Woodrow Wilson.

Statue of Thomas Jefferson

IN THE OLD DAYS

Cherokee Nation
It is thought that the ancient Cherokee Nation may have had a population of 25,000 people. Their lands stretched from Ohio to Georgia and covered an area three times the size of present-day Virginia.

Oconaluftee wood-carvers in North Carolina

Long Ago

Our journey begins 250 years ago. No, we don't have a time machine. We are going to Oconaluftee, a Cherokee village in the Great Smoky Mountains in North Carolina. Here we can watch a canoe being built and Cherokee women weave baskets and mold clay into pots. We'll find out all about the Cherokee culture passed down from generation to generation. Our guide will lead us through the seven-sided Council House and typical Cherokee homes.

Except for our sneakers and cameras, we could be in the 1700s. It's fun to pretend that we're living in the past, but it's time to move on.

Gullah Spoken Here

We're headed for the Sea Islands of Georgia and South Carolina. In the old days everyone came here by boat. But all we need to do is drive over a bridge.

Someone living on the island once told me, "Old-time talk we still de talkem here!" This is Gullah, a language that combines American and African ways of speaking. It means, "We still speak Gullah here!"

Ancestors of Gullah speakers were Africans who were kidnapped and enslaved. After the Civil War, some freed people moved to the Sea Islands. Many African ways were passed down from the elders to the children. They spoke a combination of African and English. And that is how Gullah came to be spoken here and nowhere else in the world.

Gullah Words

Tote *is a Gullah word from Africa. It means "to carry something big and heavy like a bale of hay or cotton." Did you ever hear peanuts called* goobers? *That's another Gullah word from Africa. And so are the words* gumbo *and* yambi *which mean "okra" and "yams."*

Meet an Artist

Basket making is one of the oldest crafts. Today's basket makers use some of the same materials and techniques their ancestors did long ago. The Cherokee woman pictured here is showing visitors to the Oconaluftee village how she makes baskets.

Kendra's Picks

New Orleans Jazz Festival

Every year people from all over the country come here for New Orleans's famous Jazz and Heritage Festival. Here you'll hear the sounds of jazz, gospel, Cajun, Afro-Caribbean, folk, Latin, Zydeco, blues, and more. Whew!

And then there's the food. You can taste cracklins, crawfish salad, or po-boy sandwiches made with oysters or shrimp. Then, finish your meal off with blackberry cobbler, glazed pecans, or sweet potato pie.

The Sunshine State

Now let's travel farther south to Florida, just like thousands of "snowbirds." That's what people in Florida call Northerners who leave their cold winter homes for the warm climate here. Some snowbirds are famous, such as the New York Yankees and the Los Angeles Dodgers. That's right! Some major league baseball teams come here each March for their spring training. They play friendly games together in the so-called Grapefruit League!

But Florida has more than sunshine and baseball. Listen! That's the sound of over 110,000 racing fans cheering for their favorite cars and drivers! And you can hear the roar of all those engines. We're at Daytona International Speedway in Daytona Beach. Look at all the hot cars, and this is just the parking lot. The first official car race took place at nearby Ormond Beach. The fastest car at that race set a record when it reached 68 miles per hour! Today, cars speeding around the track average twice as many miles an hour!

New Orleans

Ready for some French culture? Then let's visit New Orleans, Louisiana. Did you know that Louisiana used to stretch from the Gulf of Mexico to Canada and west to the Rocky Mountains? It was a French colony then. When the United States made the Louisiana Purchase, it doubled the size of our country.

We can see New Orleans's French history in its beautiful buildings. We can taste it in its delicious food. Feel like a late breakfast? Let's follow the crowds and order a beignet and a café au lait. That's a square doughnut and a coffee with lots and lots of hot milk. What a way to start the day!

Not only can we see and taste French culture here, but we can hear it too. Some people speak French, but not the way they speak in France. They speak **dialects** of French. One popular dialect is called Louisiana creole.

Mardi Gras celebration in New Orleans

Meet a Jazz Musician

Louis Armstrong, Father of Jazz

When Africans came to America, they brought their music with them. Here in New Orleans that music began to change. It became American. People called the new music jazz. It was an exciting time. All the sounds were new, and young Louis Armstrong was making them on his little cornet, a kind of trumpet.

Louis Armstrong first began to play music when he was about 13 years old. He loved music and studied hard. Soon, his music took him to Chicago, then New York City, and finally around the world. And everywhere Louis Armstrong went, he brought jazz with him. Some say that Louis Armstrong all but invented jazz.

Appalachia

Ready to hear another kind of music? Then let's head for the Appalachian Mountains. Families with names like McDonald and McCoy came here long ago from Scotland, Ireland, and Germany. They came looking for work and somewhere to live.

The people living in the mountains had few visitors or newcomers. For fun they sang and played their fiddles. Then someone got the idea to play country music on the radio. In 1925, a radio program called the WSM Barn Dance (later named the Grand Ole Opry) made its first broadcast. It is believed that the featured performer for the first show was Uncle Jimmy Thompson, an 80-year-old fiddler. The show became a big hit. Today, many tourists come to Nashville to see and hear live broadcasts of the Grand Ole Opry.

Have you ever heard bluegrass music? It's a kind of folk music that's played on banjos and guitars. It's very popular in this region. If you come to Tennessee in July, you can hear bluegrass at the Smithville jamboree.

Now let's travel on to our last stop. It is Atlanta, Georgia, a city with a lot of history and a big, bright future.

Meet a Country Singer

Dolly Parton

One of the mountain people who became a big star is Dolly Parton. Some of her songs are about growing up poor in Tennessee. As she says, "My real self is still in my music." With 12 children, the family did not have enough money to buy winter coats when cold weather came. Dolly sings about it in "The Coat of Many Colors." She describes how her mother lovingly made a beautiful coat for her with scraps. It was a coat of many colors. "And although we had no money—I was rich as I could be—in my coat of many colors—that Mama made for me."

Atlanta

Long ago, two American armies, one from the North and the other from the South, faced each other here. The southern army lost, and the city was burned. The people of Atlanta rebuilt their fair city. Then they just kept building. Even from here, you can see Atlanta's gleaming modern skyline.

Today, Atlanta is a major center of trade and transportation. There are lots of things to see and do here. Atlanta has concert halls, museums, theaters, and television studios. You can tour the giant CNN television studios to see how their shows are put together.

We are going to visit a quiet place. We're going to the Martin Luther King, Jr., National Historic Site. Born in Atlanta, Dr. King became a leader in the civil rights movement in the United States. As a result of this movement, new laws were passed protecting the civil rights of African Americans. This site was created to honor Dr. King and to preserve the place where he was born, grew up, and is buried.

We have come to the end of our tour. I hope you enjoyed seeing the land and meeting the people. As we say in the Southeast, "Y'all come back now!"

Martin Luther King, Jr., and Coretta Scott King

Atlanta, Georgia

Alabama

is the 30th largest state.

Population: 4,352,000

Area: 52,237 sq mi
(135,293 sq km)

Capital: Montgomery

Largest City: Birmingham,
pop. 258,500

State Bird: Northern Flicker

State Flower: Camellia

State Tree: Southern Pine

Highest Peak: Cheaha Mt.,
2,405 ft (733 m)

Arkansas

is the 28th largest state.

Population: 2,538,000

Area: 53,182 sq mi
(137,742 sq km)

Capital: Little Rock

Largest City: Little Rock,
pop. 175,800

State Bird: Mockingbird

State Flower: Apple Blossom

State Tree: Pine

Highest Peak: Magazine Mt.,
2,753 ft (839 m)

Huntsville, Alabama

Eureka Springs, Arkansas

Florida

is the 23rd largest state.

Population: 14,916,000

Area: 59,928 sq mi
(155,214 sq km)

Capital: Tallahassee

Largest City: Jacksonville,
pop. 679,800

State Bird: Mockingbird

State Flower: Orange Blossom

State Tree: Palmetto Palm

Highest Peak: 345 ft (105 m)

Georgia

is the 24th largest state.

Population: 7,642,000

Area: 58,977 sq mi
(152,750 sq km)

Capital: Atlanta

Largest City: Atlanta,
pop. 401,900

State Bird: Brown Thrasher

State Flower: Cherokee Rose

State Tree: Live Oak

Highest Peak: Brasstown Bald,
4,784 ft (1,458 m)

Everglades, Florida

Cumberland Island, Georgia

Kentucky

is the 37th largest state.

Population: 3,937,000

Area: 40,411 sq mi
(104,665 sq km)

Capital: Frankfort

Largest City: Louisville,
pop. 271,000

State Bird: Cardinal

State Flower: Goldenrod

State Tree: Tulip Poplar

Highest Peak: Black Mt.,
4,139 ft (1,262 m)

Louisiana

is the 31st largest state.

Population: 4,369,000

Area: 49,651 sq mi
(128,595 sq km)

Capital: Baton Rouge

Largest City: New Orleans,
pop. 476,600

State Bird: Brown Pelican

State Flower: Magnolia

State Tree: Bald Cypress

Highest Peak: Driskill Mt.,
535 ft (163 m)

Horse farm in Kentucky

New Orleans, Louisiana

Mississippi

is the 32nd largest state.

Population: 2,752,000

Area: 48,286 sq mi
(125,060 sq km)

Capital: Jackson

Largest City: Jackson,
pop. 192,900

State Bird: Mockingbird

State Flower: Magnolia

State Tree: Southern Magnolia

Highest Peak: Woodall Mt.,
806 ft (246 m)

North Carolina

is the 29th largest state.

Population: 7,546,000

Area: 52,672 sq mi
(136,421 sq km)

Capital: Raleigh

Largest City: Charlotte,
pop. 416,300

State Bird: Cardinal

State Flower: Flowering
Dogwood

State Tree: Longleafed Pine

Highest Peak: Mitchell Mt.,
6,684 ft (2,037 m)

Cotton fields in Mississippi

Nags Head, North Carolina

South Carolina

is the 40th largest state.

Population: 3,836,000

Area: 31,189 sq mi
(80,779 sq km)

Capital: Columbia

Largest City: Columbia, pop.
112,800

State Bird: Carolina Wren

State Flower: Yellow Jessamine

State Tree: Palmetto

Highest Peak: Sassafras Mt.,
3,560 ft (1,085 m)

Tennessee

is the 36th largest state.

Population: 5,431,000

Area: 42,146 sq mi
(109,158 sq km)

Capital: Nashville

Largest City: Nashville, pop.
511,300

State Bird: Mockingbird

State Flower: Iris

State Tree: Tulip Poplar

Highest Peak: Clingmans Dome,
6,643 ft (2,025 m)

Charleston, South Carolina

Great Smoky Mountains, Tennesse

Virginia

is the 35th largest state.

Population: 6,791,000

Area: 42,326 sq mi
(109,625 sq km)

Capital: Richmond

Largest City: Virginia Beach,
pop. 430,400

State Bird: Cardinal

State Flower: Flowering
Dogwood

State Tree: Dogwood

Highest Peak: Rogers Mt.,
5,729 ft (1,746 m)

West Virginia

is the 41st largest state.

Population: 1,811,000

Area: 24,231 sq mi
(62,759 sq km)

Capital: Charleston

Largest City: Charleston,
pop. 56,100

State Bird: Cardinal

State Flower: Rhododendron

State Tree: Sugar Maple

Highest Peak: Spruce Knob,
4,861 ft (1,482 m)

Richmond, Virginia

Petroleum works in West Virginia

Glossary

barrier island - a body of land completely surrounded by water that acts like a wall protecting the mainland from ocean waves

cargo - goods carried by a ship, airplane, or truck

coastal plain - an area of almost flat land along the sea

colony - a settlement ruled by or belonging to another country

coral - a hard substance formed by the skeletons of tiny sea animals

culture - the arts, beliefs, and customs that make up a way of life for a group of people

delta - a fan-shaped area of land at the mouth of a river. It is formed by deposits of mud, sand, and pebbles.

dialect - a form of a language spoken in a certain place or by a certain group of people

economy - how a community or country manages its resources

erode - to wear away

export - to send goods to another country to be sold

gulf - a large area of sea that is partly surrounded by land

import - to bring in goods from another country

key - a low island or reef

landform - a feature on Earth's surface like a mountain, valley, or plateau

manufacture - to make something, often with machines

marsh - an area of low, wet land

mouth - the part of a river where it empties into another body of water

plateau - an area of high, flat land

swamp - an area of wet, spongy ground

textile - a woven fabric; cloth

tributary - a stream or river that flows into a larger body of water

wetland - a low area, such as a marsh or swamp, that is very wet

Index